John Hall

Other books by John Hall

Between the Cities
Days
Meaning Insomnia
Malolactic Ferment
Couch Grass
Repressed Intimations
Else Here: Selected Poems
Apricot Pages

John Hall

Couldn't you?
Poems for pages

Shearsman Books
Exeter

First published in the United Kingdom in 2007 by
Shearsman Books Ltd
58 Velwell Road
Exeter EX4 4LD

www.shearsman.com

ISBN-13 978-1-905700-51-6

ISBN-10 1-905700-51-2

The publisher gratefully acknowledges financial assistance from
Arts Council England.

Contents

Couldn't you?   7

Gloss   11

Harder than ease   23

I on a   37

A lone knower's disavowals   38

Four topical poems   38

Here and there   41

Changing lines   49

At any time   65

An essay on lyric ethics   69

Between the fragments   75

A version of a list of giving   85

The last word   87

Notes and acknowledgements   89

Couldn't you?

In those golden days the talk was miniature and barred: understated, precise, golden and, when appropriate, just not stated at all. No voice was raised, even in silence. It was then I learnt how various omission and restraint can be and learnt to admire and envy – indeed try to emulate – articulate silence.

§

I could never get past the part in the story where they all left. A loss is not a loss unless it keeps happening. Perhaps there is a time when you are just about to lose the loss and you remember, poignantly. Like waking with a start just before you were asleep. The point is not when they left but repeating to yourself how it will be when they have gone. It will be all right won't it? No it won't. It is because you can't forget that it will happen again. Once is enough but there is no such thing as once. Once upon a time happens all the time and is impossible. It can't happen. The time which never was has gone and what repeats is not the time but the impossibility of its return except as a sense of its impossibility. What repeats is this avoidance of this story of loss. It has to repeat impossibly because it has no history. It is avoided so often it is fully there. Hung by the force of avoidance. And what hangs swings. At every moment returns to itself in order to leave for itself. It is not as though I could tell it once and for all. Though I could try. Couldn't you.

§

Despite a severance, solemnly to declare veracity and perseverance. Hit verity and back down from teeth on lips to front palate. Suppress palatal terror. Palatial errors, with flowers and vowels free-ranging over the lawns. Parkland commandeered for the purposes of modern myth. Majestic common land. Tell me I'm not wrong. Travel between vowels and prefixes through the oscillations of cut-and-run, of truth on the move. She smiles shyly because that's the way she was stolen. An old trick. If you can't say it sing it. The young charmer. More than half in love with you singing. Repetition of white teeth chanting against red lips. Truth grows delirious. Heaven knows what the doctor got up to meanwhile. Trembling in the face: teeth and lips. Paid to cure. Caring about that. Lying because you care about cure. Of course truth bleeds loss and blossom on the lips. That's the smile that severs. Spit the tooth out to say it. Why not? Truly, you'll smile later through the gap.

§

There is repetition and there is avoidance. There is avoidance of repetition. The avoidance of repetition is repeated. You don't notice perhaps because your attention voids itself, veering on to the surface of particulars. On to the line of events. This is how you love and avoid love. There is no object larger than the imagined world. Its worn corners. Its weary shoulders. Love repeats on itself. This abstraction is a loop out of the real that holes out local meaning by senseless repetition. Say it often enough and it empties. If you empty it carefully enough what is left is a fine abstraction, a void or vacuum pulling back the gravity of particulars. As though a nothing could exert such force. I repeat myself. Of course I don't. It is suspended by a force of insistence. On being nothing.

§

there is repetition
I could never get past
there is repetition and there is
I could never get past the part
there is avoidance of repetition
I could never get past the part in the story
the void dance of repetition is repeated
the lost last part in the story where they all
I could never get past

Gloss (Lyrical Abstractions)

remorse

you did it
        it
bites back

                mordant

        it bites
                it
        keeps biting

                                shame

                you wish
                you had
                n't you
                did it
                shows no
                way to
                look a
                way wound
                is
                        ever
                ywhere

guilt

wrong enough
to pay

envy

your lack
in sight o
o ther's full
ness

diffidence

hang back
(hinge)
but hanker

envy

see
   ing
      in
s
  our
      love

lust

looking to
be where
you see
there you
are
you see
you
look to see
you

envy

bad sense
looking upon

affection

facts s'
often
looks di
    late
       lassi
tude of good
ness pull
s love near
     haze
       y and you
  phoric

possession

no good
ness
when love close
s
in
on the lo
           ok to
break
    and enter

vanity

no wound in
    beauty no
end
    try in
tegrity of
end
    ptiness full
    face w'
        out depth

vanity

from a shining
surface I take
my image in air
y body my being
as in air grounded I and
you it is you
rs I have
bought it
caved in
emptor

yearning

in the eye a
fleck no
less
than a store
y of
   of loss leave
the fullness you
never had the
facts soft
end their sur
faces perm
e able

blame

speak wound o
the wise the body
im
    mac
        you
late

shame

wound
f
ills
your
eyes: I
wo
    un
        d'ed

jealousy

the image
end place: dis
face

                               melancholy

                   o
                   wo
                   und ling
                             ers
                   on wound
                   sub
                   lime half-
                             ref
                                      use half re
                   fuge
                       for
                   ge t

violence

sweet break the
im
    pos
        sible
act be
     yond sigh
 t: of   wound
        red
ness
     o
     f
o ther

irony

wound mouth
wound not
un
wound from
site
of speech

irony

point
     ed
lie be
side ever
y point: tough
e
  nough

anger

blood
breath in
he
   ad

tenderness

breath missed
ing mem
ory: you will
re
member
this

bitterness

in mouth where sweet
ness
end
   s the debt
            me
lancholy
        wo
            n't pay

Harder than ease

here   you   are
    you   see

you   see
it's   a   straw
hat

here

where

you see she

(is)

she	s
ep	he
may	may
safe	say
ly	fly
gaze	grace

hold your ardour he

hollers no love speaks

its name   it's a shame

holds utterance in

he holds ardour

at arm's length

a boulder

boards his heart

the stone that

kept the dead in

had moved

the dead do

that   you do it

for the dead

a tone meant

that he had bolstered

up his love for her

he had bouldered it in

so as not to disturb

the dead

you are you see the
dead I would mourn
had you not gone

saying you are
gone you see
you are not
gone

gone is here

this is the shape
of the vanishing
a shade
a trembling of the air

the air is mournful you see

he says heart because that way hurt

there eases

broken hearted

the vanishing trembles

in the air

where he sees from

hurts

this is lyric

and true

the hurt reels

the repeating hurt

the repealing art

the reeling real

sometimes the chant

works   heart-less

twist of words

heart lease

words turn on a wound

which is a word:

hurt

word

wound

heal

all words

hurt halts breath

dis-

ease of shallow

breathing

to say

lung-ache tho

voice hurts and heart

hammers

harder

ease

metaphor places

meaning in three

places, one

new

this can hurt

meaning is carried in breath

like flecks of TB

a tone meant, a metaphor

when breath vanishes

heart is gone

heart less ness bliss

bless

the breath

less

word

half in

love and

half of that

half

hurts   the other

half half

laugh

ter

the quarter-master's store: a metaphor from song

of where words

already are: the half that hurts

already hurt, the half-half that eases

eased before

who knows which half

a store

of very few words

more is easeful

I on a

for Peter Riley on his sixtieth birthday

"an enormous fight between 'the' and 'a'"
       "increasingly unsure whose side I'm on..."

1

Its stone is motionless in the spaces, the
theatre of moon fields. The courtesy
enclosure of scattered sky donates
something of advantage to the darkness,
momentary love towards constant loss,
lives and defeats. We retire softly
to Mansfield. The moon sets in us:
a file at the edge itself. Poor spite,
thy will be kicked by right, through
maintenance back at the bank.

2

You can bank on it, there are more
than two voices. The moon shines
on the reader of moonlight who reads
the fields the moon shines on: gifts
against darkness and for it too. It is
the nothing that shines on the edges.
It is the it that bodies the dark. (He)
reflects on reflection, electing the
elect of the moon, excitement tempered
in ordinary speech. After all, historical love
litters Mansfield and these fields.

A lone knower's disavowals

I am reminded almost every day of the story of King Lear. I am reminded of it more often than I am of the story of Oedipus, though I am a son and father and have no daughters. Others explain me to myself by way of the story of Oedipus and what I hear is Lear howling. King Lear had no sons.

At first he thought he was the only one who could say no. Certainly he thought he could say no to the daughter who could say nothing but nothing. What she said was that she had nothing to say. What he said, in his own way, was: I am the one here who has things to give; if you have nothing to say, I shall give you nothing, and my act will be the giving of nothing. The gift withheld, harboured to augment its power.

He thought he knew. And at that time he was more in control of the now than anyone. Those who know that they control the now are the ones who can strongly say no, knowing that they lose nothing. Like everyone else Lear confused power with love, thought he could give up one kind of power without abandoning the other.

No. That's what he found himself saying. No. Five times. In a row. Each one different. A howling disavowal with a continuo of nasal hum. A hundred knights so that he could retain a sense of power; the English *k* a subterfuge failing to harden the vowels that detour through the nose. The fool knows no difference between naughty and nought. Nothing hurts and is a bad night. The lone knower, powerless except for what he knows. Disavow knowledge if it hurts; sometimes known as betrayal, each way. This is the howl of know, alone, in the night. Of no, because what is now known cannot be borne. O no. Howl against knowing. Speak of nothing only when you know it.

no
o no
know now
o no now knows
one loner owes now
knows one who loans (k)no(w)
shores himself up with low moans
ekes out loss in close shaves
hovers on his ledge of (k)no(w)
peering over unsure waters
peeking at loss
losing all from show
o no
no no alone no

o no no one knows
o not now with no know-how
o no it never shows
no knower alone now
now knows how ever he raves and rolls
oh they open and
opening to no edge
she raves and rolls
she knows she not knows
unsure now of the no ledge
o no
no nouns now
show how not to know
o no

Four topical poems

map

        here

                        where

               else

                          where

thinking

        where

                     here

               where

                        else

memory

        else

                     where

                here

                        where

speaking

        where

                   else

               where

                        here

Here And There

HERE

here on the reservation like everywhere else the signs stay stop
or give way or indicate gradients in round figures as percentages
of something simpler than the scattered and wary houses in-
habited with changed wealth now that commodities that meant
lives that mean lives that means livelihoods have moved around
the globe and around technologies so that mines used to be and
now are just dangerous holes in the woods to keep out to keep
away from and the added danger too there used to be guns as
recluses guarded body space under the terse sign of ownership
hung on the entry gate as public sign of application for change
of use in this case mine is a nice pun whose are minerals anyway
now that coincidence between divinities of majesty and metal
is a hole in the wood is wool over the eyes and the wool too is
there but doesn't build churches with similar signs on the gate
though that was a city dweller's point here the churchman was
herrick who found it wet never see a gun now hear one some-
times in the woods and find the shiny plastic spent cartridges
its gates and fences boundaries arbitrary enough to sulk over
or the rivers do it the cattle grids that mark with percussive rat-
tle the sudden transition to moorland where the dark brooks
dean burn mardle and holy rise and rise fast too when it rains
changing the sounds that pass but within a scale of constancy
because what moves here stays still too and your ear catches
the rising and falling of water sounds bird sounds lowing and
calls of farm animals oil burning up and down the A38 in an-
other ribbon made of cars this time all concealing the stirrings
of separate journeys and are away in each direction down here

that's where it's reservation it keeps things as they are preser-
vation which means sometimes someone else's architecture
some other technology's way though underneath the stone or
the cedar (cedar) they are new materials warmer and cheaper
conservation which makes them worth leaving and com-
ing to and like dartmoor wood ants coming to when the first
spring sun strikes their nest heating the scattered pine nee-
dles that cover them when they come to moved and shunted
and gantried from who knows what winter stillness there has
been is now and then the ants will move out and back repeat-
edly even though it's not happening I can say it because it hap-
pens the way the river and therefore the well never dry up

BETWEEN

where is a car enclosed space german solid moving and not moving doubling at least the heres the one I'm in and the ones I pass that relativity of passage between here and there troubled with a where except when you know it so well and then the heres on the radio moving around all over the place an anecdotal world intruded heres and others that determine the cost of this journey I make its safety too do I feel safe yes and no these are not corners you can see around and some of those supposed to guard my safety scare me on this journey to and from work to home home to work as though work was still a place as it is with car parks to prove it and in both directions a cranial enclosure where I think I think ahead or behind like the old song not an adventure pitched at a future but the circuit of a repeated present pulling a future back each twist into its turns sing it again everyday knowing the rhythms stops lifts drops and turns again these rehearsals of prepositional movements and internalised imperatives leave home turn left up the hill then right watch the crossroads with the blind bend to the right and the flood too when its been raining before you see the tower of the burnt church this must be an old road to the moors from the moors to the town miss the town now these are called by-passes not to not even through by go down and right and left roundabouts painted on the road do the trick right and left and then a long run crossing the dart twice because its turns are different from the roads and left at the church thirty miles an hour on average little to do with tempo more timing not swaying to its going arriving is only temporary

WORK

this is where the church has been moved to from next to the hall where only the tower remains and placed at the side of the road where you turn from the A384 towards the hall nowhere really except in reach of the scatterings regathered under the single village name a nineteenth century twist to the feudal geography so that going to church no longer meant going up to the hall where all the economic hence 'spiritual' power had been for centuries then slipping and dispersing transforming intercepted by wealthy social and cultural idealists lavishly restoring medieval buildings and adding new modernist ones in using capital from global fuel and flight enterprises to fold back into this landscape an imagined wholeness of work art learning an integrated life asserting an end for a time of strongholds to keep strangers out far from it a court for similar dreamers and artists dispossessed by the violent consequences of racial idealism to the east across Europe so welcome to those who come to practise cosmopolitan arts in an english country garden setting they wanted to be there or they couldn't stay where they were building houses and schools and a college of arts and in one of the modernist houses seventy years after it was built I work in this feudal past in this set of structures of a revived enlightenment entrusted in the forms of entailed capital to the arts and education funded also by the state in its attempts to envisage the needs of a twenty-first century across all these times my room has a blind in it to keep the light off my eyes

NIGHT

now there is only here double curtains drawn on all the external
configurations of there a dim light encloses a here in a ritual set
of moves through reading through TV through lights off on
your back steady now and then try to turn over on to your right
curl a little cheek on the pillow always an imagined smile at this
point of emptying until there is no here either and a there enters
in dreams with a waking to a neither here nor there long before
readiness an alertness in the dark disturbing the here with later
and now and how can this have happened until sleep has quite
gone and there needs to be somewhere to go to a book per-
haps middle of the night TV don't look at the time though news
comes always as time its clock telling you more often when you
are watching than the time of what you see caught across clock
times catching you unawares time and time again with its re-
peated déjà vus is this happening now where am I seeing from
the rural dark this isn't history which is another kind of story-
time nor one of those fictions which take over time the birds
and planes are hushed though somewhere news is breaking into
time as it passes we'll bring you updates while you sleep bagh-
dad delhi where I am it says where I am is dark is anywhere
the satellite reaches like where you are sleeping I hope what
can you do with these non-dreams of others what's the score

WRITING

heart felt a scattering and a gathering heart ease the heartlands
the veldt these artisan processes whose conflicts hurt first take
these graphs and make of them a sentence why it is a very long
way from sentence to letter parse it down no further it is graphic
and heart felt and you don't know if this is something you saw or
heard what you hear are parsed pauses breaking hearts in many
places again and again and as you tease this out you wonder if
it is the same place of damage here place is a sound and a vague
shape in your body about which you can sometimes say here it
is just here and that it hurts or you hurt as soon as you say you it
is all of you a whole place for others say that you hear nothing in
these circumstances except a sob one sob say and it all goes qui-
et it may or may not be you sobbing it may be a he or a she who
sobs and it may be a one who sobs and so an it and that it is not
quite you though your heart is not as quiet as the room is when
you think this because everyone in the room replays that one sob
in anticipation stopping their breath but not their hearts a letter
cannot escape the heart by way of the mouth except in transla-
tion a phoneme can it is as though a letter a single letter had
escaped because that is what a sob is a single sob it is an escape
from the body of one person that might enter the body of oth-
ers vague and translated just below or above speech more of an
escape than a sigh is though perhaps a little further from speech
do you see how letters do not stay silent despite your best efforts

who speaks who doesn't who knows here that speech isn't wanted even by herself himself see how the genders switch in the air of these imagined speakers who need another story when we have always had too many which is the same as not enough and all they do is say that this is how it is or this is how I say it is or this is how it could be the moods switching around even more than the gender proscription knowing when you should keep your mouth shut your writing fingers still although at this point it wouldn't occur to some to speak and it wouldn't occur to others not to do you practise not speaking what you cannot let out hold it there is that the same as hold it in what is it to speak aloud to nobody that body that is not you at least yet who is listening in when you write when will they hear you this is not a letter except one to nobody or everyone or that letter to a someone withheld or with the proper names all switched I am writing there is nothing ahead I am circling there is something below or within these are sentences heartbeat heartfelt words not sentences fuel and shape like john wayne in the searchers cold hot heart look what avoidance has done stiffening hardening returning to the practised distances of childhood fearing your touch exactly because I want it and in this sentence I don't even know who you are a touch in general somewhere no longer the touch of a named someone and this is the age-old story of age troubled memories of bodies aged thirty in their dreams

Changing Lines

Slightly smaller ...

Slightly smaller
All have red crowns
Whitish belly
Isolated black streaks
Seldom drum
Both parents share in care of brood
Resident

These centuries of the decline of ancient philosophy
Almost forgotten
The task of gathering and ordering the entire corpus
Quite natural for them
Logic, physics and ethics as their guiding thread
Hand down material not put in question

There can be no plagiarism in philosophy
A permanent type of the speculative temper
Nature as a mirror or reflex of the intelligence of man
The impress of reason
Living energy of an intelligence
Experience has gradually saddened the earth's colours for us

Could you ever say I don't want to hurt you without hurting
Pain-killing a typical metaphor
Morpheus was the Roman's god of sleep
Of quick-sand dreams
This love vague and necessary
These things that I do to show that I am here
Mourning the loss of bed-warmed skin
A device for carrying distance over sound
A ritual act against night fear of incompetence

Pray for the competence of prayer
Speaking about to begin, about to end, where blessing comes

Margins without pages
Your words give off the others you know nothing about
A listening you can assign to the dead if you wish
Your solitude is strangely companionable
You have crossed through loneliness to the other side
You have to go back, with ink in your mouth
You miss the nameable dead horribly
There is no one to tell
Your tongue moves in solitude
This could be called talking to yourself

You cross over again
You rejoin the dead if they will allow
Only as you speak to yourself
You speak for them
You speak because of them, out of loss too
Grieving the previous dead
And all the time you are blind, your rainbow eyes

You should sleep you would like to sleep
You find that you have behaved badly in another's dream
Something you do that you will not say that you do
A lover – actual or desired – hovering over your exchanges
Fails to protect hurtful data

The impress of reason...

The impress of reason
Speaking about to begin, about to end
Ritual act against night fear
Something you do that you will not say that you do
So your tongue moves in solitude
Praying for the competence of prayer
Slightly smaller
Pain-killing a typical metaphor
Resident
You rejoin them if they allow
Only as you speak to yourself
Seldom drumming
Margins without pages
Logic and ethics as a guiding thread
Living energy of an intelligence
I should sleep I would like to sleep
Hand down matter not in question
Isolated black streaks
There's nothing to say
I don't know that I don't know who I am
How should they love you
All have red crowns, almost forgotten
Helplessly wrong-doing in another's dream
Experience saddens the earth's colours
(With)draw your words
Prized as share of blood

your words give off...

Your words give off others you know nothing about
    Your solitude is strangely companionable
       You have to go back, with ink in your mouth
        Your hair stands on end
         You speak for them
           You speak because of them, grieving the previous dead
          This love vague and necessary
           Mourning lost bed warmth
           You miss the nameable dead horribly
           Rejecting all consolation
           You don't know who you are
           You have crossed through loneliness to another side
           And in quick-sand dreams
           You fail to cross over again
           Would you ever expect not to be hurt
           Usually a simple moment
           Quite natural
           Where you could say the dead are
          Whitish belly
         What if you said I do want to hurt you
        This could be called talking to yourself
       There can be plagiarism in love and its knowledge
      These things that I do to show that I know and love
     Nature as a mirror or reflex of Intelligence
    There is no one in your solitude to give
The prize of gathering into one place your entire body

A listening you...

A listening you can assign to the dead if you wish
    draws your words
        a lover – actual or desired – hovers over each exchange

This machine carries distance over sound
    ritual act against night
        and all the time you are blind, your rainbow eyes

You keep saying I don't want to hurt you
    even this thought hurts
        experience has gradually saddened the earth's colours

Hand down material is not put in question
    I don't know that I don't know who I am
        I should sleep I would like to sleep though not

Helplessly a wrong-doer in another's dream
    writing its black line
        those quick-sand dreams impossible

Always on a margin
    mourning the loss of bed warmth
        nature as a mirror of intelligence

As you speak to yourself
    using pain-killers in typical metaphoric fashion
        praying for the competence of prayer

As they move in solitude
    blessing comes quite naturally for them
        something you do that you will not say that you do

Your tongue is a solitary mover
    alone in its cave, protecting and rejecting data
        the impress of reason

There can be no plagiarism in solitude
    or else it is a knowledge copied endlessly
        this task of gathering and ordering

The known solitude of your body
    is gathered from others in acts that mirror love
        how should it know or love

There is no one to tell
    these centuries of the decline of ancient thought
        these things that I do to show that I am here

Talking to myself no mirror mists over
    these are two uneasy lovers
        not reducible for a moment

To ear and tongue
    the others keep returning in vague and necessary love
        you cross over again

You don't know who you are
    though as they enter and you love them
        really you don't know that you need to know this

You have crossed through loneliness on both sides
    where you find the others who love
        and where you say the dead are

You miss the nameable dead horribly
    each time you have to go back, with ink in your mouth
        you speak because of them, grieving even their previous dead

Your solitude is strangely companionable.

This machine...

This machine carries distance over sound in a
   ritual act against night
and all the time you are blind, your rainbow eyes

Hand down material is not put in question
   I don't know that I don't know who I am
I should sleep I would like to sleep

A listening you can assign to the dead if you wish
   draws your words
a lover – actual or desired – hovers over each exchange

You keep saying I don't want to hurt you
   And I can see that this thought hurts
Experience of hurt has gradually saddened the earth's colours

Helplessly, a wrong-doer in another's dream
writing its black line
those impossible quick-sand dreams

Always on a margin
mourning the loss of bed warmth
nature as a mirror of intelligence

Your tongue is a solitary mover
alone in its cave, protecting and rejecting data
the impress of reason

The known solitude of your body
is gathered from others in acts that mirror love
how should it know or love

You don't know who you are
    though as they enter and you love them
really you don't know that you need to know this

As you speak to yourself
    you use words as pain-killers
and pray for the competence of cure

There can be (no) plagiarism in solitude
    though barely audible knowledge whispers endlessly
always gathering and losing a drifting corpus

There is no one to tell
    these centuries of decline of ancient thought
these things that I do to show that I think

You have crossed through loneliness to a place
    where other lovers talk silently
of the dead they say they find there

You miss the nameable dead horribly
    each time you have to go back, with ink in your mouth
you speak because of them, grieving even their previous dead

As they move in solitude
    blessing comes quite naturally for them
something you do that you will not say that you do

Talking to yourself no mirror mists over
    these are two uneasy lovers
not reducible for a moment

To ear and tongue
    the others keep returning in this vague and necessary love
you cross over again

Your solitude is strangely companionable.

The prize of gathering...

The prize of gathering and ordering an entire body

                     so your tongue moves in solitude

and your words give off others you know nothing about

                     living energy of Intelligence

you have crossed out loneliness

                  this is how they should love you

your whitish belly

Experience has gradually saddened

                     your speaking of them

you cross over again, expecting to be hurt

                you should sleep you would like to sleep

dreams and metaphors augment your pain

              you miss the nameable dead horribly

an impossible drumming

You don't know

                     you mourn lost warmth

your solitude is strangely companionable

                  isolated black streaks

there is no one to tell

                   no one resident

there's nothing to say

                              usually a simple speculative movement

impress of reason

                                  this is vague and necessary

your rainbow eyes.

And all the time you are

                              where you could say the dead are

you have to go back

                                  ink pours from your mouth

in dreams of the quick

Nature as a mirror or reflex of the intelligence of man

                                      your guidance threads

quite naturally

                                        but you know

only copies of love and knowledge

Your hair stands on end

and all the time...

and all the time you are
be
    coming blin
                dly impossibl
                        e,   a machine
forgoin
        g distance, lover
how your
jailor's eyes
keep tabs on speculative
listening
mum's the word
no
other
place for the
quietness of you dead who
rest in
silent
threat
under co
        ver of
whitening bone.   e
                    xperience pales before
your pri
        zed silence

At any time

1

at any time
a dynamic
of psychic
and social
forces
violence
around the edge
of peace or
comfort
all the forces
that lean in
are sanctioned
no one threatens
on the street
I work and live
where this is unlikely
it is not my choice
to have this choice
genealogical centuries of being on the right
side of the usually unspoken
argument
those who design
and manage the protocols

for collective behaviour
distribute supplements
conceive and apply sanctions
for default
and if I live
apart
it is not apart
from this disposition
that makes apart
both desirable
and possible
unspoken power
that hardly
even whispers
to me

2

that hardly
heated argument
even whispers
rammed apart
unspoken power
lest at any time
edging around the edge

sanctioned

in extremis

siding with the

usually unspoken

order ratified

distributed as supplements

every choice

rare comfort

of those who administer

no one threatens

escaping from this disposition

so genealogical

since it is not apart

the protocols on the street

o this my

negation of choice

even forces

such a dynamic

edging all the forces

leaving centuries of right

where I work and live

peering on the side

ever sociable

re-entering the possible

so that leaning on me

or making apart

negates no violence

An essay on lyric ethics

a circuit of economics belief territorialism
a competition for the right to resources
a desk of my own
a lyric elegy for a damaged world
a noble violence
a political life-cycle of fuel
a roll call of names
a space of arbitration and withholding
a violent anti-violence of writing
a word with dance in it like chorus
an ineradicable violence

and to resist damage
anyone who isn't for us is against us
apostrophe is dramatic not lyric
as ontological destiny
as part of their job

behind me beside me above me
bracketing out particularity
but these should not be confused

can lead to systematic mass murder
constellated by coincidence into systemic evil
costing lost sexual violence

dispersiveness

epic song
everyone needs to know who deserves
expensive solitude
extend beyond any lyric instance

for players of musical instruments
from the ethics of lyricism

geared teleology
genealogy of comfort

having nothing to stand under
helped death workers see themselves as noble
however ceremonially restrained

I keep the company of the articulate dead
implicit violence of any belief
implies a world of the possible
in a denial
in certain circumstances
in most circumstances
in my solitude in my negotiations
in notorious examples
in the conditions of a poem
instances of individual pathology
is a condition

is certain and figures
is dangerous
is it enough that
is love or war
is lyric always melancholy does it need
is not caught up
is this sentence one of 'ours'
its surface inscribed

love takes the named as its object
lyric mobility

modal possibilities

named as a 'war on terror'
not just a competition for resources

of corporate extermination
of course there are 'bad apples' at home
of the dramatic
of the nameable
of the purity of sameness
of the right to inflict damage
of what it could be to be human
only one of which
or perhaps where drama hands over to lyric
or this terminal with its abstract address
overseen by images of male ancestry

part pensioner part employee
points at the name-holder's chest
power outpowers power

say that each poem
sitting at a desk indirectly bequeathed
spreading freedom
stories accounts poems and arguments

take a simple lesson
take the names away and I speak foolishly
tempting into place a theology of devolved absolution
temptingly nameable
that a poem's linguistic order
that certain poems
that freedom is a right
that gives me title
that right is a freedom
the American people
the articulate absent
the mechanics and performances of power
the motor car for example
the nameable is destroyable
the right to damage in the name of this right
theologians used to know this
these conditions of lyric personae
these epic conditions of lyric solitude

this new expensive pen

this world in which evil is abroad

those who murdered

though as ever names double as decoys

though I have no doubt

through its exclusion of certain

throughout the world

to adopt the posture that humans do when they sing

to catch an erotics of will a violence of drive or purpose

to ignore and deny damage

transcendent subjectivity

uncertainty of circumstances

up against

waived the death sentence

we want each other('s)

what contract of belonging

where music and poetry are concerned

where resources are always subject to contest

wishing for a better world

within a territorialism of style

within the complexity of financial regulation

within the law

yes ok co.uk

Between the Fragments

to have these

        stepping forward

records, to say

        from my hand, and

there was

        at his own breast

this, &

        would knock

this

        tradition

it was not always

        We then tried

as it is

        called out

of all this

                  him to send

and cared nothing

                  return of post

in the Endymion

                  mail, but no

on the

                  opening

search

                  nothing

active duty

                  and the sage

over

                  abroad

jabbers English

before I could

America there is no

as much as these

these respects

readily, in

I had

expectation

to break

reflect

logical friend

so tardy

quite as

myself

impress is required

        America in command

language

        of the first things

us, and I

        copies of

the truth

        Spanish

more words

        title

method

        Displayed

firmly

        o Man

To have these records! He jabbers of all this in English, stepping forward before I could send him to America, and cared nothing, saying there was this and this! Suppression is required. It was not always as it is. There is no return from this post of 'as' language – as much as America is in command at these my hands, and in the mail; but no 'us', and of the first things I, Endymion, pay these respects as readily as though they were copies of his own truth and would knock on the opened Spanish breast. I had circled more words with titles, with nothing. My interference breaks tradition in this respect. Active duty, my logical friend: we then tried a display of retarding method, but were over sagacious. This man quite firmly called out to myself: come abroad.

under the flower

ing hands of the mid

shipman in my charge

under my chest with my love I recce'd

walking in green, mended

by light showers and

the pink flowery skin of several officers,

white by our choice.

I applied to them all

saying, whether we flee ourselves

or force a study of the Spanish

main hope is our full method

second argument

the big ship moves the ordinary manipulations
past. there was in the course of service
mist. the ship went the wrong
way, lacking instrumentation, and I do not choose
to go faster with my tongue

though I love speed, security
comes from sound observation and attentive
leadership. far behind the scene
she finds once in a Spanish port
where war gives qualified welcome to certain strangers
a Scottish lieutenant

we strolled along the path which overlooks
the town of Corunna
every peasant saluted us

an ally may be loved ceremoniously but is not necessarily a friend
I know you only by the help of my books; fog
placed under cover the original English dispatch

we observed a wine-house crowded with people
thinking this a good opportunity for studying manners
we entered; the landlord
stepped forward with a cup of his best beverage
of course we drank to the health of Ferdinand the Seventh which
appeared to please them amazingly, for they all shook hands
with us in turn as we took leave

third argument

so this 'war'
'with the world watching'
of course we would not be expected to doubt this
everybody makes connections
'from our own leaders'
'no one' doubts he is a vicious leader
'trust me'
the essential commodity of modernity
to be killed by your own prophet (profit)
'rogue state'
the FTSE is up because of early war successes
more damage was expected to oil supplies
these 'events' are 'our top stories'
time changes its rhythm, its pitch, its attack
so you notice anyway
or you do if someone tells it
makes perhaps a disconnection
so what's happened with you
everything that has happened has always happened
stories swallowing their own throats
you don't notice
threats are stories of stories that might happen
would happen if it weren't for this make-it-happen
'hallucinations are facts too'
'terrorists' threaten the 'freedom' of just watching thank you
we'll bring you more on this story as it unfolds
alternative energy sources
on your knees before an 'act of god'
explicitly excluded from your schedule
but as for you, that's enough

fourth argument

as much observing war as at war
he was twenty
at thirteen entering the navy
his father gave him a notebook
sailor-writer
a Scottish lieutenant in Corunna in 1809
that's the kind of story called history
is that all we need to know about power
looking ahead
what to do with the power crazy
when power is marked out ahead and in another place
as a place of resourcefulness
how does duty play in this
the referred calling – ie the call of the sea
may not in the first place
be a call to war
the erotics of ritual power-display
of course clothes are weapons too
in Corunna he goes to the opera
clothed to be desirable
he is my great great grandfather
as such I test him out
somewhere in the forelife of narcissism
'I cannot help remarking how different,
and yet how much alike, the same person may be
at different periods of his life; how much changed
in thought, in sentiment, in action!'

A version of a list of giving

a break
a compliment
a damn
a piece of my mind
a toss
and take
any price
as good as she got

away
birth to
blessing
chase
cold shoulder
consent
credit
ground

head
in
into custody
it up
~~let him have it~~
my bond
my heart
my word

myself to
of my own free will
off
one last chance
out
over
place
rise to

sentence
substance
the command
the time of day
their lives
this man
this woman
thought

time
tongue
up
vent
way
what he had coming
what I have
you that

The last word

Sorry is the last word in the long lost dictionary.
            (Barry MacSweeney, "Up a height and raining")

Exposure makes for concealment

Better than anything the masked tone

I'm sorry I'm so sorry

Something I didn't know I'd done

I am sick writing and thinking this

Anger would have made things easier

But you must say it properly

And look it as well

Something goes out of you

Sorrow fills the place of this loss

I am angry may not be angry enough

Something has come into you

Pained at heart, distressed; full of grief or sorrow

A sorry state from which you might say calm up

What our shadows seem, forsooth, we will ourselves be

Sorge, a German word, apparently translatable as worry

Things that you do with others

Do I look like that? you think me that: then that I am

I write on ice

A shift in the ratio of the described to the undescribed

A swing door: swish – sorrow; swash – anger

Sorry, we are closed.

Acknowledgements and Notes

Some of these poems or versions of them have appeared in or on *Oasis*; *Shearsman Gallery*; *CCCP 12* (Cambridge Conference of Contemporary Poetry; publication withdrawn); *April Eye: Poems for Peter Riley*; *Tremblestone*; *Great Works*; *Jacket*; *Starting at Zero Review, Don't Start Me Talking: interviews with contemporary poets*. My thanks to the editors and publishers. Sadly, in the case of Ian Robinson, editor of *Oasis*, these thanks are posthumous.

'I on a'.

There is a well known category of gift, which relies on the recipient to make available the means of giving. The quotations are from one of the letters at the beginning of Peter Riley's *Alstonefield*. The title and the first stanza are made up entirely – give or take some minor morphological liberties – from words found in the first seven stanzas of the same book.

'A Lone Knower's Disavowals'

"The prose section of this piece accompanied the first version of 'A Lone Knower's Disavowals', a set of framed visual poems shown in *Loose-idity*, an exhibition of the author's work (Dartington Gallery, 2002). A photograph of the frames hung together on a single wall can be seen on the Shearsman website (http://www.shearsman.com/pages/gallery/john_hall/disavowals.html). The prose appeared again on the back of a folded insert of an A3 version of the same pieces in *Poetry Quarterly Review* N° 20 (Summer 2003). My thanks to the curators and editors."

'Between the Fragments'

Sources:
Captain Basil Hall (1831) *Fragments of Voyages and Travels, Including Anecdotes of a Naval life: Chiefly for the Use of Young Persons*, Vol

II, Edinburgh: Robert Cadell;
John Hall (1968) *Between the Cities,* Lincoln: Grosseteste.

'A version of a list of giving' was prepared for *Partly Writing 4*
which took place in Bury, Lancashire, in June 2005.

www.ingramcontent.com/pod-product-compliance
Lightning Source LLC
Chambersburg PA
CBHW030047100426
42734CB00036B/549